Everything You Need to Know About

SCHOOL VIOLENCE

Violence is increasing everywhere, even in schools.

• THE NEED TO KNOW LIBRARY •

Everything You Need to Know About

SCHOOL VIOLENCE

Anna Kreiner

THE ROSEN PUBLISHING GROUP, INC.
NEW YORK

Published in 1996 by The Rosen Publishing Group, Inc.
29 East 21st Street, New York, New York 10010

First Edition

Manufactured in the United States of America.

Library of Congress Cataloging-in-Publication Data

Kreiner, Anna.
    Everything you need to know about school violence / Anna Kreiner.
— 1st ed.
      p. cm. — (The need to know library)
    Includes bibliographical references and index.
    Summary: A thoughtful discussion of violence in schools, complete
with examples of incidents and suggestions for coping.
    ISBN 0-8239-2054-2
    1. School violence—United States—Juvenile literature. 2. School
management and organization—United States—Juvenile literature.
[1. Violence. 2. Schools. 3. Weapons—Safety measures.
4. Safety.] I. Title. II. Series.
LB3013.3.K74 1995
371.5′8—dc20   94-24121
                                                       CIP
                                                         AC

Contents

Graffiti is a fairly common form of violence.

Introduction

*C*harlie and Jim are walking to their lockers. "So," Charlie says, "was that my girlfriend you went out with last night?"

Jim starts to laugh. "She sure likes me," he brags.

Charlie's voice gets angry. "You leave her alone. I don't want anyone stepping on my ground. If you know what's best for you, you'll stay out of my way."

Jim laughs. He thinks Charlie is joking. "What are you going to do?"

Suddenly Charlie pulls a knife out of his pocket. Jim turns and runs down the hall. He trips. Charlie reaches out to stab him.

Another student tackles Charlie. Soon the teachers and the principal surround him. The school guard takes Charlie away.

Jim stands up and brushes himself off. He is scared but not hurt.

Jim is lucky. He survived the attack. But not every student is so lucky. Today many students have more to worry about in school than exams and strict teachers. School has become a dangerous place.

Students are encountering violence in school.

Feelings like jealousy can spark an outbreak of violence.

What Is Violence?

Violence is the use of physical force to cause harm.

Violence in schools can take the form of crimes against property or persons. Destroying school property or spraying graffiti on the school walls are examples of the crime of vandalism.

Some students steal money from teachers or other students. They go through desk drawers or break into lockers. Others steal computers, typewriters, and expensive lab equipment.

Vandalism and violence are wrong. Students and teachers can't use textbooks that have pages ripped out of them. School districts have to pay to repair damaged classrooms or desks and to buy new supplies. If they don't have enough money, the students and teachers are hampered in the process of education.

An even more serious form of violence is the use of physical force to hurt another person. Sometimes a violent person strikes out with hands or feet. But today more young people are carrying knives and guns. They use these dangerous weapons to hurt or even kill their teachers, principals, and classmates.

In recent years school violence has become more common and more deadly.

What causes violence in school? How can you protect yourself? What should you do if you are a victim? Is anyone trying to stop this violence?

This book will help you understand why violence occurs in school. It will tell you where you can get help and how to protect yourself. Violence is frightening. But the more you know about it, the better prepared you will be. Then you can do your part to make your school a safe place.

Even your peers who seem happy may be facing violence and stress at home or in school.

Chapter 1

What Causes School Violence?

Shawna was furious. Mom wouldn't be home until late tonight. Shawna had to make dinner for her three little sisters, wash the dishes, and do all the housework. "Why do I always have to do everything?" she grumbled.

After she had finished, Shawna took out her math homework. She wasn't doing well in math, and there was no one at home to help her with the assignment. "I'll see if I can do it," she muttered. "But I wish someone would help me. I'm tired of trying to take care of everything myself."

Then her friend LaDonna called. In tears, LaDonna said she thought she might be pregnant. Shawna listened for a while. Then she told LaDonna she would try to help her figure out what to do tomorrow.

Shawna went back to her desk and scowled. Tears streamed down her cheeks. This was the last straw. She was totally overwhelmed. She had too much to do and no way out.

She was furious with the math teacher, Mr. Crawford. Why did he have to give such tough assignments? Shawna had more important things on her mind.

Tomorrow she would show him.

Shawna knew her mom kept a gun in the bedroom. Mom said she wanted it to protect her family from criminals in the neighborhood.

Shawna took the gun from Mom's nightstand. Now she felt powerful.

The next morning Shawna walked into math class. When Mr. Crawford went to the blackboard, Shawna stood up.

"No more stupid assignments for me," she said. She pointed the gun at Mr. Crawford and pulled the trigger.

The bullet hit Mr. Crawford directly in the chest.

Someone screamed. Then people started running everywhere. The principal ran into the room. Soon a police car pulled up outside the school.

An ambulance rushed Mr. Crawford to the hospital. But it was too late. He died on the way to the emergency room.

Crime on Campus

The use of weapons is definitely on the rise in the U.S. Despite public support for gun control, access to guns is relatively easy. And an increasing number of students carry guns and other types of weapons, such as box cutters, to school. Many

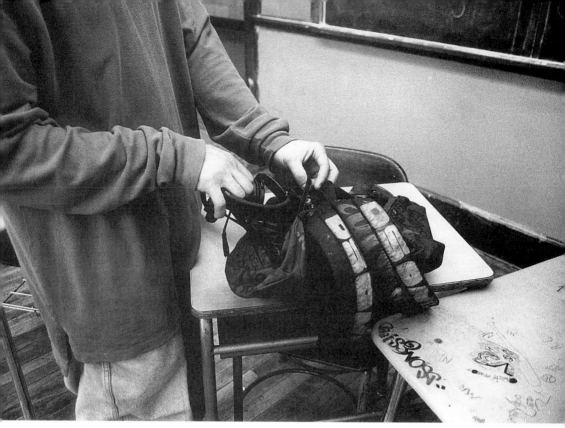

Many students carry weapons in the same casual manner in which they carry Walkmans or notebooks.

teachers and students now believe that their schools are unsafe.

- Every year 3 million thefts and violent crimes occur on or near school campuses. Once every six seconds a student or teacher in the United States is the victim of a crime.
- During the 1980s, 11,000 people died as the result of high school youths carrying guns.
- A national survey found that at least one out of five students and one out of ten teachers have been victims of school violence. If you are in a class of thirty students, that means that six of your classmates are likely to be hurt by violence during the school year.

13

- Metal detectors and security guards have been placed in some schools. Despite this precaution, violence continues.

Students and teachers have been hit, stabbed, kicked, or shot. Sometimes a single student is the attacker. Sometimes groups of students gang up on a teacher or another student. In one urban school district in New York, nearly 100 teachers have been assaulted by students each year for the past four years.

The most common occurrences tend to be disagreements between individual students. The least common form are attacks by gangs of students against teachers.

Although most of the aggressors and victims are male, female students also carry weapons and act out physically. And bystanders, male or female, also are hurt when students use violence.

As a result, more than three quarters of American teenagers believe that threats of violence are a problem in their schools.

And recently more than 80 percent of the nation's school districts reported that violent crime had increased during the past five years.

Is School Safe?

"Give me your money—or else." This might sound like a scene from a back alley. But

Violence is found everywhere, even in lyrics of popular songs.

unfortunately the speaker was a junior high school student in Wisconsin. It is not an isolated case. Almost 40 percent of the nation's eighth-graders have been threatened with violence. And almost one out of five has been injured at school.

Schools should be a safe place for learning. When someone is afraid, he or she is not able to learn as well. Fear reduces that person's ability to be a good student. Unfortunately, more than one third of the students polled in a recent survey said they were afraid at school. Violence in the school means that students are not learning as well as they can.

One high school in New York City reported

51 violent incidents in 1993. At another school, a 19-year-old female student struck the principal over the head with a bottle of soda. At still another high school, a 17-year-old student was charged with trying to rape a 15-year-old in a classroom after school.

A survey found that one out of 12 students stayed home from school for fear someone would hurt them or hassle them.

Parents and teachers are afraid too. The National Rifle Association (NRA) polled parents on what they thought about gun violence. Almost one third of the adults said that they worry about gun violence when they send their children to school.

Do you feel safe at your school? Being afraid makes it hard to learn. How can you concentrate on your lessons if you are worried about getting hurt?

Violence also makes it harder for teachers to do a good job. They have to spend more time disciplining students. They may be distracted from their teaching if they have fears for their safety. Some teachers have even given up teaching because they were afraid of violence in their schools.

Many people used to think that school violence was a problem only in city schools. During the 1970s, for example, teachers in urban schools were nine times more likely to be attacked than teachers in rural schools.

Many cities do have serious problems. There are more guns, drugs, gangs, and crime in urban areas than rural towns.

But that has begun to change. In 1978 the National Institute of Education published a report for Congress stating that school violence is a national problem.

During the 1980s teenage gun deaths in suburban and small towns increased for the first time.

A researcher at Texas A & M University found that boys in small Texas towns carry handguns to school at twice the average national rate.

A 19-year-old student was convicted of first-degree murder and sentenced to life in prison without parole. He fatally shot two people and wounded four others on the campus of Simon's Rock of Bard College in Massachusetts in December 1992.

And a recent study revealed that violence is a problem in schools across the country, regardless of the size, location, or ethnic makeup of the student body.

School Violence in the Past

Kids have always broken the rules in school. Most of the "bad apples" caused trouble by talking out of turn or being late for class. They were discourteous or disruptive. But they were not usually violent.

Some students did cause serious problems. During the 1800s educators and lawmakers began to recognize that juveniles do commit crimes.

Instead of treating these students as adult criminals, they set up special courts. More important, however, they established reform schools to try to help them.

Sometimes the reform schools did help students to become more responsible members of society. But more often they just kept them off the streets until they became adult criminals.

In the 20th century, legislators, teachers, and the public have had different opinions about school discipline and violence. In some periods teachers have emphasized "progressive education" and a relaxation in strict discipline. If they thought students were getting away with too much, they tried to reimpose stricter standards.

The 1950s and 1960s saw many changes in society. People began to question authority, particularly when it seemed racist or sexist. Students stood up for their rights in a way they had not done before.

Many young people liked these social changes. They didn't have to submit to the rules and strict disciplinary policies of the past that many thought were unfair.

But some people think that the relaxation in school discipline was a mistake. They blame the current rise in school violence on lax rules. If students think they can get away with violence, these people argue, then they will act out.

These people believe that public schools should have strict regulations and be allowed to expel troublemakers. They believe that the schools are the problem.

Many private schools have high standards that public school teachers envy. "Students in the private schools realize that if they don't live up to the standard of the school, they will have to leave," said one public school teacher.

Our Violent Society

Why does school violence occur?

There's no easy answer to that question. Part of the problem certainly lies in American society. We live in an increasingly violent country.

You turn on the radio. You read the newspaper headlines. What's likely to be at the top of the news? Another murder. A drive-by shooting. A report of domestic violence or a rape right in your neighborhood.

In 1992, almost two million violent crimes were committed in the United States. Twenty-three thousand people were murdered. One hundred thousand women were raped. And more than one million people were victims of assault and battery.

In 1992 the Surgeon General of the United

Sometimes what you wear or carry can trigger a violent reaction in someone else.

States declared that injuries and deaths from gunshot wounds had become a public health crisis.

Today, gunshot wounds are the second leading cause of death among all children of high school age. Murder is the leading cause of death among young black men. The homicide rate for black youths nearly doubled between 1984 and 1988.

Teenagers are more likely to be the victims of violent crime than adults. Out of a group of 1,000 teenagers, 67 will be victims of violence each year. Among 1,000 adults age 20 or over, 26 will be victims of violent crime.

Murder, crime, and theft are now commonplace in too many cities and towns. The gates of the schoolyard can't keep these problems out. So it's not surprising that many teachers and students experience violence in the classroom.

Gangs and Drugs

Jeff knew he had made a mistake. He had worn a red sweatshirt to school. That was the color of one of the gangs at school. Now they would be out to get him, assuming he was baiting them. Jeff put his knife in his pocket. He hoped he wouldn't have to use it, but he was ready.

It's easy to get involved in gangs. Selling drugs and making big money can be tempting, especially when you need money fast. Joining a gang may also seem like a good way to belong. Gang life may seem glamorous and exciting from the outside, but it's very dangerous.

"I have to carry a gun," said one student in a Los Angeles school where gang violence is common. "If I don't have a weapon, how can I protect myself from the guy who does have one?"

Almost all gang members have been victims of violence or know someone who has. Many innocent bystanders have been victims as well.

In addition, drug use by teens can result in greater violence at school. Someone who is high is more likely to behave impulsively. It is easier to hurt someone else or take risks when high on drugs. A drug addict may also steal from other students or teachers to pay for his habit.

The Changing Family

But gangs are only part of the problem. Most school violence is not gang-related.

Some people believe that the rise in the number of single-parent families has led to an increase in school violence.

"Parents either don't have the energy or the desire to teach their kids values," they say.

But not everyone agrees with that view. "My mom taught me the difference between right and wrong. It was important to her, so she made time to do it," says a boy who grew up in a crime-ridden section of Los Angeles.

Other people think that the breakdown of the nuclear family has led to violence by creating greater stress for parents and children.

Many parents work long hours. They have little time to spend with their families.

Students like Shawna often have to take on many responsibilities at an early age. Sometimes they feel overwhelmed. When they get angry or frustrated, they may lash out physically.

Young people who face an empty house or apartment at the end of the school day may be lonely and upset. Others, whose parents seem too busy to pay attention to them, feel unloved or

Parents are working longer hours, and more teens face the responsibilities of being alone.

unsupported. Some of them join gangs for friends and excitement. Others become angry loners. They may use violence against the people around them.

Students and Weapons

School violence doesn't require a weapon. But when weapons are readily available, violence becomes more likely.

More than half of the students in grades 6 through 12 polled in a recent survey said they could get a handgun if they wanted one. And most of those students thought they could get it within a day.

One student in twenty carries a gun, according to a study
by the federal government.

"Getting a gun? No problem. I'd just 'borrow' it
from my dad," said one student.

An inmate at a juvenile detention center said he
could get one fast and cheap "off the street."

Our society is full of weapons. Private citizens
own more than 200 million guns.

The federal government conducted a study to
find out how many students carry weapons. The
result: One student out of 20 carries a gun.

Another survey found that almost one quarter of
the students responding had taken a weapon to
school during the past month. They carried the
weapon either to protect themselves or to use in a
fight.

The widespread violence and crime in America
contribute to the violence in our schools. But just

as important as the occurrence of violence is our attitude toward it.

Many young people learn early in life that violence is okay. Our society and sometimes our families accept violence—and sometimes even promote it.

Children who grow up in homes where there is domestic abuse think violence is a normal part of life.

Many violent people were abused when they were young.

Young people who are abused or who see other family members abused often lash out themselves. They become violent because they are angry. Sometimes they use their fists because they don't know any other way to solve their problems.

"I didn't know my dad shouldn't hit my mom," said one young woman. "I thought that's how everyone acts."

A youth was sentenced to four years in a juvenile detention center after he brutally attacked a younger classmate.

"That's how my stepdad got us to do what he wanted. I figured the same way would work for me," he said from his cell.

Violence and the Media

Even young people who grow up in homes without violence often learn that violence isn't bad.

Movies, television, and radio frequently blur the distinction between violence and entertainment.

Think about your favorite Saturday morning cartoons. How often does one character blow up another while everyone laughs?

Which movies are the biggest box-office hits? Usually the most violent.

From the early Westerns to today's cop thrillers, Americans have loved to watch the heroes and the villains put up their dukes and fight.

Even if the good guys do win in the end, they usually use violence to get there.

These programs and movies tell viewers that violence is okay. It will help you solve your problems. And you might even have fun doing it.

Young people often imitate the characters they

see on television and in the movies. Very young

children may have trouble distinguishing fact from fantasy.

"I didn't know it would hurt him," said an eight-year-old boy after he was arrested for beating his next-door neighbor. Even older students who know that violence can hurt may try to act like their heroes. Some students try to capture the entertainment value they get from the big screen by acting violently in real life.

Movies, newspapers, and television don't deserve all the blame. They are sending a message that they get from the rest of society. For instance, if fewer people went to see violent movies, film makers would soon make fewer violent films.

Recently many Hollywood producers agreed to limit the amount of violence in their movies and television shows. The law limits the amount of violence that can be seen on programs aimed at children. But many young people are still getting the message that there is a place for violence in our society.

Unfortunately, violence in school often leads to more violence. Even nonviolent students may carry a weapon for self-protection.

John is a good example. On the news it was reported that in six months school guards had confiscated nearly 100 weapons from students.

"One hundred guns and knives?" thought John. "My school must really be unsafe. I'd better start carrying a weapon to protect myself."

Chapter 2

Getting Tough at School

*B*eep, beep, beep. Steve walked through the *front door of his high school. He heard what sounded like a siren. Then he knew: It was a metal detector.*

The school guard walked over. "Empty your pockets," he said.

Reaching into his backpack, Steve grabbed the knife and raised it to the guard's face. He wasn't going to give in without a fight.

The guard quickly knocked the knife out of Steve's hand. Then a policeman read Steve his rights. He was under arrest.

Weapons in School

You have probably walked through a metal detector in an airport or a federal office building. But some students now encounter them on a regular basis—in their schools.

You can't necessarily tell which students are armed in school.

Because of the upsurge of violence in the U.S., the federal government and some states have passed strict weapons laws. In most states, it is illegal for anyone to sell a gun to anyone under 18. The laws also forbid anyone to carry a concealed gun without a permit. In 1990 Congress passed a law making it a felony to have a gun within 1,000 feet of any school. Ten states have passed laws that make adults responsible for leaving guns where children can get them.

But students still take guns to school. And the law doesn't cover other weapons such as knives, razors, clubs, or brass knuckles. Students in Texas have even begun to carry metal hair combs with sharpened teeth.

Too many students use their fists as weapons.

More schools are hiring security guards and installing metal detectors. Almost 15 percent of the nation's school districts use metal detectors.

If the detector reveals that a student is carrying a weapon, the school guard or police officer confiscates the weapon. The student then may be arrested. Other school districts reprimand, suspend, or expel students for weapons violations.

Shape Up or Ship Out

Mr. Stanford had had enough. All week Karl had been interrupting class. Mostly he just talked out of turn. But yesterday he had loudly threatened another student, and today Mr. Stanford saw a knife in Karl's desk. It was time for action. Mr. Stanford called the principal and sent Karl to her office. The principal telephoned Karl's parents and told them that their son was suspended for three days. Then she told Karl that he would be expelled if he ever brought a weapon to school again.

Many teachers complain that student misbehavior interferes with teaching. They want stricter rules and better enforcement in their schools. Some school districts have responded by imposing new disciplinary procedures. Students who commit violent acts may be suspended or expelled. In some states juvenile delinquents are sent to prison camps, detention centers, or alternative schools.

Some reform schools help students with behavior problems learn new ways of coping. But critics claim that many alternative schools are discriminatory "dumping grounds." They say that minority students are overrepresented and that the schools don't help the students at all.

Some districts can't afford alternative schools. So violent students either stay in the system or get no education.

Charles was new to Santa Monica High School. He didn't have many friends. Some of the students were afraid of him. He was sullen, and all he liked to talk about was his dad's gun collection.

One day during lunch period Charles started to beat Mark. He injured the boy so badly that Mark had to be taken to the hospital.

Charles was arrested. Then the teachers learned

Some educators believe that parents should take a more active role in disciplining their children.

that he had been arrested before and expelled from his old school because of his violent behavior.

The angry teachers wished they had known about Charles's record. But in their state the court records of juveniles are kept secret.

Students' Rights and the 'Get-Tough' Attitude

Teachers are worried about their safety and want more information about violent students. In many states the records of juvenile offenders are sealed. The court system protects the rights of young people by keeping this information private.

But teachers say they have a right to know

about students who are prone to violence. In 1989 California adopted legislation requiring school districts in the state to inform teachers about students who had hurt or tried to hurt another person.

The American Federation of Teachers, the nation's second largest teachers' union, wants more information-sharing. It believes that violence can be diminished if students who might act out are identified early and receive special attention. Not everyone agrees, however.

Some schools are trying to reduce gang-related violence by prohibiting students from wearing clothes that are often associated with gangs—for instance, certain types of hats, pants, sneakers, sweatshirts, and jogging suits—to school. Since fights sometimes break out because a gang member thinks another student is wearing the "wrong" clothing, many teachers and students think this is a good policy.

Others believe it doesn't go to the heart of the problem, since gang-related violence makes up only a small part of the crime in most schools. They also think such rules unfairly restrict students' freedom of expression.

Many teachers and students approve of the stricter atmosphere in their schools. "It's time for someone to teach these kids a lesson," says a California teacher. "We've got to get back the discipline that's gone out the window."

"I feel safer knowing someone's looking out for

us," says a student at a Maryland junior high that recently installed metal detectors.

But other people oppose the use of metal detectors and security checks. They believe that these methods violate students' rights.

In Detroit, the American Civil Liberties Union and the school district worked out a compromise. The district agreed to tell students in advance before they installed metal detectors and to use them only where there was a problem with guns.

The teachers want the parents to become more involved in the schools. In some districts parents have joined the "get-tough" movement, patrolling the hallways for weapons and violent behavior.

Some educators believe that parents need to take a more active role at home too. They want parents to teach self-discipline to their children and support the school's disciplinary procedures.

Many people think the "get-tough" attitude helps. They believe students use violence just because they think they can get away with it. Do you think stricter rules make students stop hurting others?

What Else Will Stop the Violence?

Metal detectors and stricter police protection can help to reduce the violence. But some students still take weapons to school. They learn how to hide their guns, knives, and box cutters.

And students will always have at least one weapon—their fists.

A more important part of solving the problem is to help students recognize that violence is unacceptable. They need to realize that it won't solve their problems and that its consequences can be very serious for their victims and for themselves.

As long as students think violence will help them get what they want, they will continue to hurt other people and property. By challenging students to reconsider their attitudes toward violence, schools and parents can help to make long-lasting changes.

Sometimes people use violence because they feel overwhelmed by their problems. Some don't like themselves. And some are angry with the world around them.

The next chapter discusses how schools are trying to change the way students think about violence and to help the students manage their problems. Educators are teaching students about the dangers of weapons and violent behavior.

Chapter 3

Changing How We Think About Violence

*T*he students stand in front of the judge.

Yesterday the two boys were arguing about money. Each one claimed the other had stolen $10 from his locker.

They began to scuffle in the schoolyard. Before they became violent, the teacher on duty broke up the fight. Then she told them they would have to see the judge.

But this judge isn't wearing a long robe. She's not sitting in a federal or city courtroom.

The judge is another student. She's sitting in a school classroom.

Students Helping Students

Many schools like this high school in Maryland have introduced *peer mediation* to reduce the violence in their classrooms.

Many schools have turned to peer mediation to solve disputes between students.

These programs help students resolve conflicts before they become violent. The mediators are students who have been trained to listen carefully and offer fair solutions.

Each student presents his or her side of the story. Then the mediation team draws up an agreement for both sides to sign.

Getting Extra Help

Schools used to be places to learn the three R's—reading, 'riting, and 'rithmetic. But now many are adding a fourth R—relationships.

Most violence occurs between people who know each other, not strangers. So it's important to learn

Drug and alcohol abuse among teens is rising. It is likely that this is contributing to the rise in violent behavior.

how to talk to the people you know and solve your problems with them without using violence.

For most teachers in 1940 the most serious student problems were talking out of turn, chewing gum in class, and making noise.

Today, many students have more serious problems. A similar survey in 1980 found that drug and alcohol abuse, teen pregnancy, and violence were at the top of teachers' lists.

Educators know that students face many challenges outside of school. When you're worried about gangs, drugs, and alcohol in your neighborhood, it can be hard to feel safe anywhere. And sometimes students take out their anger and frustration on the people around them.

Counselors and teachers want to prevent violence before it happens. So they are teaching students nonviolent methods for reducing stress and dealing with anger.

"I used to use my fists when I got angry," says one student who has been suspended four times for violent behavior. "Now I'm learning to talk about what bothers me."

At a school clinic in Alabama, students can get extra help to cope with drug and alcohol problems and family stress.

Local businesses, churches, and community centers are also trying to help young people find alternatives to gangs, drugs, and fighting.

"I went gang-banging because there was nothing

There are several people you can turn to if you have a problem with drugs or alcohol.

else to do," says one youth at a community center in Milwaukee. "Now I know that at least one night a week I can come here to play basketball and have some fun."

Forming Relationships

There is another important reason why focusing on relationships can help to reduce violence. Many criminals feel no connection to other people in their lives. They look at other people almost as objects. They forget that the person at the other end of the knife blade or gun barrel has feelings too.

Researchers have found that adolescent murderers tend to be not only violent, but extremely violent. One teenage murderer stabbed his victim 46 times.

A psychologist who studies violent teens believes that these young people feel very bad about themselves. "For a person to treat his or her victim like a piece of meat—I believe you yourself have to have been dehumanized."

These violent teens often don't care what they do to themselves or to anyone else. When you feel good about yourself, you are less likely to use violence.

Thinking About the Consequences

Schools are also helping students to consider the direct effects of violent behavior.

Most people imitate the behavior of those around them. If your friends smoke, you probably smoke too. If your friends see violence as an acceptable way of dealing with things, you may begin to see it that way too.

Former gang members in Los Angeles and other cities talk to students about gang life.

"Yeah, it's cool and exciting," says one former gang member. "And you can make money. But that's only good if you're alive."

Almost all gang members have been involved in violent activity by the time they've been in the gang for four years.

Former gang members know that it's not a good idea to bet on getting out before the violence starts. "You never know when the guy in the next car will pull an Uzi. It could be tonight."

But gang-related and drug-related violence are only part of the problem of school violence. A student is more likely to be shot by another student during a feud about a boyfriend or girlfriend or a disagreement over possessions than to be shot by a gang member.

In some places students are starting to think about the consequences of their acts. Violent students lash out to get what they want. They don't think about what will happen afterward. When they recognize what they've done, they feel sorry.

A Boston reform school is trying to help violent youths develop better problem-solving skills. They are learning to think of alternatives to violence.

The teachers ask the students the following question:

Another kid has the last ball on the field. You want to play with it. What do you do?

Getting a part-time job will not only give you a sense of respon-
sibility and a place to belong, but it will teach you valuable skills.

The first reaction of many students? Hit the
other student and take the ball.

After going through a special problem-solving
program, more students came up with a new
answer: Play catch.

Students are also learning how dangerous
weapons can be. This type of education has to
start early. Most weapons-related crime occurs in
high school—but almost one quarter of the gun-
related violence takes place in junior high. Guns
have even been used in preschools!

A New Outlook on Life

Another way schools are trying to reduce the
violence is by giving students hope.

"What difference does it make?" said a teen in a high-crime area of a large city. "If I don't shoot them, they'll shoot me. And probably someone else will shoot both of us anyway."

Unfortunately for many youths, violence has become a way of life—and death.

They don't believe they have a future. They do not expect to get a job or live in a safe neighborhood. So they find it easier to go along with what's happening at the moment. And often they use violence to get what they want right away.

Schools try to help these students by giving them skills they can use to get a good job. They also help them plan for a successful future.

Jerome used to hang out on the street corner in the afternoon. He was lonely and bored. A few times gang members asked him to join. Jerome was tempted. There were no jobs in the neighborhood. And the guns the gang members carried looked exciting.

Jerome almost gave in. But his story has a different ending. His school and community center joined together to form a youth program. Every day after school Jerome went to the center for a recreation and job skills program. He and the other teens started a small business selling school supplies. And they had a safe place to have parties, play sports, or just talk with their friends.

Soon Jerome will graduate from high school. "The program came just when I needed it," he says. "I

*liked the other guys. And the counselors were cool
too. We worked hard, but we got results. And when I
go out in the world now, I know I have the skills to
find a good job."*

Programs like these can help reduce violence.
They give teens a good feeling about themselves.
And they prepare students to make it in the real
world without hurting themselves or anyone else.

In some community centers and schools, youth
leaders who grew up in the neighborhood talk to
young people about how they changed their own
lives. They help the students stay in school—and
stay safe.

School violence will decrease when students
recognize that it causes more problems than it
solves. Sometimes using your fists or a weapon
seems like a good way to get what you want right
away. But it doesn't help in the long run.

In this chapter you have read about how
teachers, community leaders, and families are
working together to stop the violence.

Many people are trying to find solutions. How
can you stay safe in school? What can you do to
prevent violence? The next chapter gives some
answers to those difficult questions.

Chapter 4

What You Can Do

What can you do to be safe in school?
You know that violence is a problem in many
schools. Knowing about a problem won't make it
go away. But once you are aware that it exists,
you can figure out ways to make it less of a
problem.

The most important step is to learn how to
protect yourself in a violent situation. But you can
also help to achieve a larger goal: preventing
violence before it happens.

Protecting Yourself

How can you protect yourself?

First, listen to your instincts. If you feel unsafe
or uncomfortable in an empty classroom, hallway, or
in a particular section of the school grounds, pay
attention! Try to leave or find an alternative route if
you can.

One way to protect yourself is to avoid looking like a victim. Carry yourself with confidence and pay attention to your surroundings.

Also, pay attention to your surroundings. Is someone walking uncomfortably close behind you? Don't just pretend you don't notice; do something to try to increase the distance between you. Is it in a crowded hallway? Surround yourself with people, or turn abruptly to the side so that the stream of people will carry the threatening person with it. Is it on your walk home? Go into a store. Stay near the cash register. Don't be afraid to tell the manager that you think someone may be following you.

If you see a student with a gun, knife, or other weapon, tell someone! But do so carefully so that the student will not know who reported it.

Tell a teacher, the principal, your parents, a guidance counselor, or another adult. If you don't feel you can tell the adult in person, write a letter. There is no need to sign your name.

You are not responsible for taking the weapon away from the other student. It's usually not a good idea to confront the other person, especially if you are alone. Let the school officials or police take care of the situation.

If someone threatens you with a weapon, it is usually best not to fight back. Do what the person orders, and then report the incident to the authorities.

Suppose you are in the schoolyard, and Joe swaggers over to you. "I'm going to get you," he says. "I may not bring my gun to school, but there's nothing to stop me from using it later. Watch out." What should you do?

If anyone threatens you, tell a trusted adult right away. Just because you won't be on school property doesn't mean the school staff doesn't want to help you. They can notify the police and your parents, who will help you to stay safe.

It's important to remember that violence does not require weapons. Try to avoid confrontations with students who might threaten you with their fists or feet.

For instance, if you get angry with someone, don't use insults or name-calling. It might feel good at the moment, but you are likely to make

You can learn effective ways to protect yourself by taking a self-defense course.

One way to avoid potentially violent situations is not to use drugs.

the other person angry. If the two of you become involved in a physical fight, you may both get hurt.

It's important to talk about your anger. If you think you can have a reasonable conversation, tell the other person in a nonthreatening way what he or she did and why you feel angry.

If that does not seem possible, talk to an adult or a trusted friend. They may be able to help you deal with the other student. Even if you decide not to confront the person who made you angry, your new listener will help you handle your anger constructively. That way, your anger will not simply build up inside you.

Do your best not to get involved in violent situations. If you can, walk away from anyone who threatens you, especially if the person has a weapon. If you can't, stay calm and try to negotiate your way out of a potentially violent situation.

It's not a good idea to fight back even in a fistfight. Walk away if you can. Don't use violence just to save your pride.

Use physical force only when you can't get away and you think you will be in greater danger if you don't fight back.

Learn effective ways to protect yourself by taking self-defense classes.

Never take a weapon to school. Violence is more likely to happen when a weapon is available. If you get angry, you might be tempted to use your knife. If you don't carry a weapon, you'll have time to think before you act.

You may think you need to carry a weapon to defend yourself. But too often the weapon is used against the person who carried it, even if he or she had it only for self-protection.

Helping Yourself

If you think that *you* are likely to become violent, there are several steps you can take to help yourself.

First of all, never carry a gun, knife, or other weapon.

Stay away from gangs and drugs.

If you tend to feel like using violence when you

get angry or feel overwhelmed, talking to someone else can help. If you don't want to talk to your parents, try a guidance counselor, an older brother or sister, or a friend. Youth leaders and clergypeople also are good listeners.

Your listener may not be able to solve the problem directly. But just knowing that someone cares about you can make you feel better. And that person may recommend other people who may be able to help you. Then you will be less likely to react to your problem in a way that will hurt someone.

Think before you act. Shootouts may look exciting in the movies. But after the scene is finished, the actors put away their fake guns and go home for the night. If you shoot someone with a real bullet, your story won't have a happy ending.

Will violence solve your problems? You might think that hurting a classmate who's been bugging you will get rid of the problem. But what about the next time someone irritates you? You can't use your fists to fix everything that's wrong.

If you use violence, you're likely to cause more problems—for your victim and for yourself.

Stop Violence Before It Happens
You can also work to prevent violence before it happens.

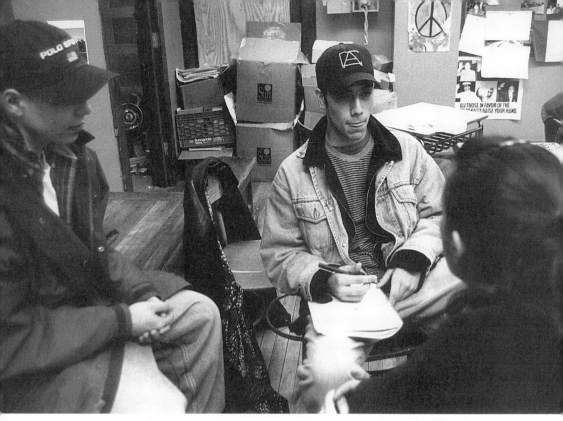

You might join or start a support group or a group aimed toward finding ways to stop violence in your school.

One way is to start changing how you look at guns and violence. Don't act impressed if someone shows you a weapon he or she has brought to school. Don't encourage your friends to use their fists when they get angry.

Do your friends like to hang out in places where there's a lot of violence? Suggest other things to do—playing sports or listening to music. You and your friends might also choose not to watch violent movies or television programs.

You can help your friends when they get upset. Tell them you want to listen to their problems and help them. Discourage them from getting involved with gangs.

You walk into science class in back of Manuel. Joseph sticks out his foot and trips Manuel. Manuel glares at Joseph. Then you hear him say, "I'll meet you at 3:00 out back. You know what for."

You know that Manuel and Joseph fight a lot. And they usually get violent. What should you do?

Tell an adult that you think there will be a fight after school. Then the adult can take action.

Suppose you don't know ahead of time that there's going to be a fight. But as you're leaving school, you see a crowd in the schoolyard. Manuel and Joseph look angry. They're starting to throw punches. What should you do?

Get an adult right away. Don't encourage them to keep fighting. A fight may be exciting—but it's excitement with a high price.

Don't try to break up the fight yourself. You might be seriously injured.

Those are some things you can do by yourself. But you can also work with other people to reduce school violence.

Working with Others

Talk to school officials and community centers in your area. Maybe you can organize an after-school club or recreation time.

A nonviolent life doesn't have to be boring!

Your community center might set aside time for you to play sports or have parties.

If the staff members know that people in your school are interested in these activities, they will be more likely to help you get what you want.

Do you want to be a peer mediator? Talk to your principal or guidance counselor. One of them may be able to help you start a program.

Talk with your friends about how you can feel safer in school. You might organize an after-school support group. Drugs, alcohol, and fights with a boyfriend or girlfriend are hard problems, but you can get support from people who are having the same experiences.

You can be a role model for younger students. Sometimes kids copy what their older friends or relatives do. When you say no to violence, you are setting a good example for them.

You might want to become a "big brother" or "big sister." Everyone needs someone to listen. Maybe you turned to a close friend or an adult; now you can do the same for your friends or relatives in the lower grades. If other students in your school are interested, you can form a "big brothers/big sisters" club.

You'll help your little "brothers" and "sisters" by showing them that there are better choices than violence. You'll help yourself at the same time. Being a good friend will make you feel better about yourself.

Shawna was 14 when she shot Mr. Crawford. She

Students who feel good about themselves don't need to use violent behavior.

spent the next four years in a juvenile detention center. Soon she will be released.

"I can never get back the years I lost," she says sadly. "I can't believe what I did. I should have thought before I acted. I'll live with the guilt for the rest of my life. All I can do now is make sure that no student or teacher ever suffers like Mr. Crawford did."

You can do your part too. School violence is scary, but each of us can help.

It's important to get rid of weapons. Guns, knives, and box cutters are dangerous.

We have to change how we think about violence.

Hurting other people or stealing from them doesn't solve your problems. And violence is not glamorous. It may seem exciting, but the results are deadly.

Students who feel good about themselves and close to the people around them don't need to use violence. And when you can look forward to a good future, you won't lash out with your fists or destroy school property.

Students, teachers, and parents are working together to prevent violence. Together we can make our schools a safe place for everyone to learn.

Glossary—*Explaining New Words*

aggressor   Person who attacks or threatens another person.

confiscate   Take away property.

domestic abuse   The use of violence or hurtful words by one family member against another.

juvenile delinquent   Young person who breaks the law.

mediators   People who listen to both sides of an argument and help find a solution.

nuclear family   Mother, father, and children who live together in one household.

reform or **alternative schools**   Schools for young people who have broken the law.

vandalism   Destruction or damaging of property on purpose.

violence   The use of physical force to cause harm.

weapons   Guns, knives, pipes, or other items used to cause injury or damage.

Where to Go for Help

In the United States

American Civil Liberties Union
Check the phone book for your local chapter.

Education Development Center, Inc.
55 Chapel Street
Newton, MA 02160

Center to Prevent Handgun Violence
1225 I Street NW
Washington, DC 20005

National School Safety Center
4165 Thousand Oaks Boulevard
Westlake Village, CA 91362

National Victims Resource Center
Box 6000-AJE
Rockville, MD 20850

In Canada

Canadian Civil Liberties Association
#403, 229 Yonge Street
Toronto, ON M5B 1N9

Canadians Concerned About Violence in Entertainment (C-CAVE)
167 Glen Road
Toronto, ON M4W 2W8
(416) 961-0853

Victims of Violence National Inc.
Unit 2, 220 Mulock Drive
Newmarket, ON L3Y 7V1
(416) 836-1010

For Further Reading

Blue, Rose, and Nader, Corinne J. *Working Together Against Hate Groups.* New York: Rosen Publishing Group, 1994.

Hull, John. "The knife in the book bag." *Time*, vol. 141, no. 6, February 8, 1993, p. 37.

"The issues" (rise in incidence of school violence). *Congressional Quarterly Researcher*, September 11, 1992, v. 2, no. 34, p. 787. Sarah Glazer has written several useful articles on school violence in this volume.

Landau, Elaine. *Teenage Violence.* Englewood Cliffs, NJ: Julian Messner, 1990.

Nordland, Rod. "Deadly lessons." *Newsweek*, March 9, 1992, volume 119, no. 10, p. 22.

Schleifer, Jay. *Everything You Need to Know About Weapons in School and at Home.* New York: Rosen Publishing Group, 1994.

Toch, Thomas, and Silver, Marc. "Violence in Schools." *U.S. News & World Report*, November 8, 1993, p. 30.

Index

About the Author
Anna Kreiner was born and raised in the Philadelphia area
and received a masters degree in public health from the
University of California at Los Angeles. She works as a
free-lance writer.

Photo Credits
Cover photo, pp. 49, 51 by Michael Brandt; pp. 26, 42 by Katherine
Hsu; p. 32 by Lauren Piperno; all other photos by Yung-Hee Chia.